Dare To Do

IMPERFECT

Stop Doubting Yourself And Go After What You Want

JIMMY ASUNI

Dare To Be

Imperfect

Stop Doubting Yourself And

Go After What You Want

Jimmy Asuni

Dare To Be Imperfect: Stop Doubting Yourself And Go After What You Want

ISBN: 9781096764809

Book Design & Book Writing Coaching & Publishing done by:

Brand for Speakers
www.brandforspeakers.com

Table Of Contents

---- ★ ----

Praise For The Book

‒ ★ ⭐ ★ ‒

"As a motivational speaker, I highly recommend "Dare to Be Imperfect" for anyone who feels stuck in their life. It is an easy, good humoured and engaging read. Offering clearly outlined steps that will help anyone achieve their life goals. It was impossible to put down, and packed with inspirational gems that give everyone knowledgeable rewards. Jimmy Asuni captured the essence of living life to the fullest for every generation to enjoy."

Jaina Ford, CEO of X2Cme, LLC
Public Speaker, Narrator and Producer,
www.x2cme.com

‒ ★ ⭐ ★ ‒

* ★ *

"Jimmy Asuni teaches us that we can all achieve our potential and reach greatness regardless of our personal circumstances, or where we are in life. Through Jimmy's incredible life-journey, we learn how to overcome adversity, break through fears, and achieve any goal that you set your mind to. Jimmy is a true inspiration, and his passion, great knowledge and wisdom are collected within his step by step guide "Dare To Be Imperfect "- a powerful lesson to us all."

**Steve Frew -
Scotland's First Gymnastics Commonwealth Games Gold Medallist, www.SteveFrew.co.uk**

* ★ *

"Such an incredible book by Jimmy Asuni, what I really enjoyed is how he has elevated himself out of doubt and into alignment with the true being that he is, which has provided in depth content in how to accept where you are and go after your dreams, not allowing any social labels to restrict your success. A must read for those who have a dream to achieve!"

Hermione Sihukai

* ★ *

Foreword By Harry Sardinas
Public Speaking, Empowerment and Leadership Coach

Jimmy Asuni is one of the most inspirational motivational speakers I have ever met. He has achieved a lot more than many people dream of because of his enormous determination and enthusiasm. Many would have given up a long time ago, yet he decided to keep going.

He is one of the most well - presented motivational speakers I have ever seen, and everything about what he does doesn't cease to amaze me.

I highly recommend listening to Jimmy Asuni especially if you are someone who is struggling to get the motivation to achieve daily tasks.

Jimmy is an entertaining speaker and he sets a great example for people with disabilities. It took him a long time to get accepted to work in a bank, and yet he never gave up. He applied to as many banks as it took to get the job. That says something about his character, his personality and his drive in the face of adversity.

As a public speaking coach, I empower people to fulfil their full potential with my international public speaking and branding workshop called www.SpeakersAreLeaders.com.

I am inspired by Jimmy's passion and I am confident he will create a ripple effect of transformation in the world with the power of his speaking.

I invite all of you to buy his book and come to his

workshops because he is incredible.

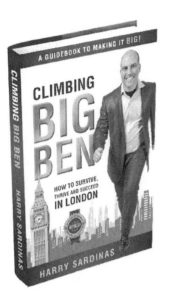 

About The Book

Every day, as we live our lives, we are inundated with images of perfection. They're on billboards, on television, in films, and perhaps especially on social media. How many times have we seen examples of someone's "perfect life" on Facebook and Instagram?

And do you know what? Most of it isn't even real! Photographs are staged, images are filtered or manipulated, and what we are being presented with is a story – a fiction – that conveys the message the person wants to get across. Very often, the aim is to get you to buy something.

Here's where it gets destructive; many of us feel that if we, and the lives we live, don't measure up to the fake perfection we are presented with, then we are failures. All of this pressure to be perfect is making people feel depressed, anxious and inadequate.

That's where this book comes in. *Dare To Be Imperfect: Stop Doubting Yourself And Go After What You Want* is the antidote to the pressure to be perfect. It's a guide to help you realise that you can succeed on your own terms – even if you aren't Insta-perfect.

If you have ever been told you can't achieve your goals in life, if your self-talk – that little voice in your head – has become negative, if you feel like a failure, if you feel depressed, unloved and discouraged, then this is the book for you.

In it, I share some of the tips and techniques I have learned and developed over the course of my life that have helped me to achieve success – despite not being perfect. The essence of my message can be found in my blueprint to bring out the best in you. Every day, aim to become a little wiser, stronger, more self-aware than the day before. Stop competing with other people and start competing with yourself. Learn to be your own best friend, reinvent your future and live a life without limits.

You don't have to be perfect. And yes, you can be successful – you, just as you are.

★ ★ ★

About The Author

Jimmy Asuni has faced challenges his whole life long. He was born with cerebral palsy. That's a broad term used to describe a group of chronic disorders that impair coordination and control of movement, due to damage to the developing brain.

The first time Jimmy realised the impact it had on him was when he'd been videoed playing football. When he watched the tape, he could see how differently he moved, compared with the other youngsters who were playing. It immediately affected his self-esteem, as he felt he was "less than" other people.

That hard lesson was hammered home when he started at primary school. Children can be cruel, and his classmates immediately latched onto Jimmy's disability and mocked him for it.

When Jimmy was just fifteen, life dealt him another savage blow, when his beloved dad was killed in a plane crash. That's a loss he still feels deeply to this day.

Despite this, he stuck with school and completed his education to secondary level, after which he moved from Nigeria to the United Kingdom. As his father was British, it felt like a natural thing to do.

Once in the UK, he embarked on tertiary education. He completed a number of courses and achieved a business management degree at London Metropolitan University.

Unfortunately, life hadn't finished with Jimmy yet. A series of bad experiences plunged him into depression and he fell into the habit of self-medicating with alcohol. His family and friends did what they could to help and, eventually, he went to see a doctor. That finally set his feet on the path to recovery. His family and friends kept on encouraging him to continue, and to inject some colour into a life he felt was grey and drab.

Around this time, Jimmy found his faith. He had been listening to a lot of Christian preaching on the Internet, when one sermon in particular had a huge impact on him. It totally transformed his dream and vision for his life and helped him to be more consistent in his approach to things.

Despite the many adversities Jimmy has faced, he has always been ambitious. He wanted a better life for himself than he had – he just didn't know how to get it. It was when he was at rock bottom that he realised the true value of his own existence.

Jimmy was at the point of wanting to end his life. He literally had a knife in his hand, ready to do just that, when the realisation that with God, all things are possible, hit him. He saw that life is too wonderful to waste, and dropped the knife. From that point on, he decided to live differently and he set out on a journey of self-awareness and self-improvement.

The key learning points of that journey are distilled in this book.

It is his ambition not only to have a better life for himself, but to help others be the best they can be and live their own best lives, too. He is living proof that adversity can be overcome and that even in the darkest moments, hope can flourish. It is this story that he wants to spread and share, so that as many people as possible can benefit from his experiences and transform their own lives, as he has transformed his.

★ ★ ★

Note To The Reader

My life hasn't been easy. I have been through it all – from abusive relationships to having to work with people who have their own unhelpful agendas and work against you. The cerebral palsy makes things a little harder, with all the aches and pains in my joints. It hurts on most days, but I keep going because I don't want to let my loved ones down. Most importantly I don't want to let myself down.

Depression is real. My depression is real. I have had to hold on to my faith in dark moments to get through it.

My life when my dad was alive and now that he's gone are two different stories. I miss my dad and I wish he was still here. If my dad were alive, he would make sure he had everything under control.

I can't even begin to tell you how much I learnt from him, he was such a cool man. He was the man that could draw the family together. He loved his family and friends and used to go out of his way to make sure everyone was okay. He was everyone's friend; I wish I had grown up with him by my side.

I owe a lot to my mum, too. She was also a huge influence on my life, and taught me to read and write.

Death is a strange thing and can have an impact on people's lives in ways you can't imagine.

There was a time I thought my life was over, because I had made a lot of mistakes. However, I learned that your mistakes in life are not the end of life; they are there to make you grow. And, if you continue to make mistakes along the way and fail, it doesn't mean you are a failure – it just means you haven't found the way to succeed yet.

Every person who has achieved success in life has experienced rejections, failures and bad times. You should never give up – through your difficulties you will eventually find the light within and shine like a diamond. I promise you, if you keep at it and get all the necessary help along the way, you will succeed. Never give up on what you want in life. Keep going for it. If you aim for the sky and don't hit it, at least you will hit a star.

Acknowledgements

Thank you to Lily Patrascu for helping me publish my book and getting my ideas organised.

I would also like to say thanks to my family and friends, who have helped me through the tough times.

I have so many people to thank that I would not know where to start, but you all know who you are. Your support and love through the years have made me strong.

Dedication

I would like to dedicate the book to my late father Olujimi Asuni.

Chapter 1
Unleash Your Inner Power

Whoever you are, whatever you want to do in life, it seems there's always someone keen to tell you that you can't. Well, I'm here to tell you that you can. It won't be easy, it will take hard work and courage, but – no matter what your imperfections, challenges or circumstances are – you can achieve your dreams.

How do I know?

I'm living proof.

I was born with cerebral palsy, which is the name for a group of conditions that affect coordination and movement. Muscles can be weak, movements can be jerky, development can be slow, and it can cause problems with sight, touch, speech and the ability to swallow. There's no cure, but there are treatments and therapies that can help.

Just like everyone else, I had dreams and aspirations, and I made the decision that I wasn't going to let my condition hold me back. I realised that I had to find the ability in my disability, and I'd encourage you to do that, too.

For example, people told me I could never be a motivational speaker because of my speech impediment – but guess what? I'm doing it, regardless. I'll tell you more about that, later.

I am here to encourage you, and to tell you that, no matter who you are, no matter what obstacles you face, you can live your dreams. You just need to tap into the wonder within.

You have the power ...

Your Dreams Are Yours.

Don't Give Up On Your Dreams.

INNER POWER
Mastery

1. MOTIVATION
2. INSPIRATION
3. PLANNING
4. ABILITY
5. MOMENTUM
6. OPTIMISM
7. REBOUND
8. REINVENTION
9. TRANSFORMATION
10. PASSION
11. GOAL-GETTING
12. AUTHENTICITY
13. ACTION

You Have The Power To Change Your Circumstances

As you journey through your life you will try to do many different things. Some might work out exactly as you'd hoped, first time, whereas others might take more effort. It's up to you, as an individual, to make the most of every opportunity that comes your way.

That's my philosophy, and I live it every day.

Despite my disability, I bought a house and I'm able to live on my own.

I've got qualifications that I studied hard for and that now open doors for me.

I enjoy speaking to and motivating people.

I'm incredibly passionate about giving back to people, to help them achieve their dreams. I especially enjoy helping people who think they can't achieve what they want – I love opening their eyes and their minds, I love seeing that moment when they realise that actually, yes, they can achieve their dreams.

Nobody is a failure – I know that to be a fact. If you tried to do something new and it didn't work out the way you'd hoped, that doesn't make you a failure. On the contrary, it makes you a trier, and you should keep on trying until you find the right resources.

Everyone has heard of the Ford Motor Company. It was founded by Henry Ford, who became an immensely wealthy man, a business magnate and philanthropist. Surely no one would call him a failure! And yet, Henry Ford had to try a number of times before he found success – for him, the third time was the charm. Had he given up after the first or the second attempt, he'd barely be a footnote in the annals of history.

So, be like Henry Ford. Learn from things that don't work out – then try again, all the wiser for the lessons learned.

You Are Born To
STAND
OUT.

You Have The Power To Be Inspired

Be open to what other people are doing and saying. One or another of them is likely to harmonise with your own way of thinking and to give you the inspiration you need to keep going forward, towards your dream.

We all benefit from a little inspiration. Whatever you find inspirational has the power to be motivational – that's the turbo boost you need to find success.

You Have The Power To Inspire Others

As well as being inspired by others, you have the power to be their source of inspiration. Sometimes you meet someone who is exactly who you need; other times you meet someone and you are exactly what they need.

My aim in life is to inspire people through my story and my message that you can overcome adversity to achieve your dreams.

I want people to learn something new about me and what I have achieved, and to realise that can apply to them, too.

I want to be able to inspire others through my book and my programme, so they can learn from me, and turn that knowledge into positive action in their lives.

That is why I created the Inner Power Mastery System that is a blueprint for you to follow so that you too can achieve your dreams, regardless of obstacles and adversities. This system is broken down into parts in the following chapters and I am hoping it will inspire you to follow your dreams.

In The Pursuit Of Your Dream,

You CATCH IT, You CARRY IT, And Then CONVEY IT.

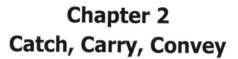

Chapter 2
Catch, Carry, Convey

One of the most powerful routes to success is a three-step process that I'm going to share with you now. The three steps are:

- Catch – your vision
- Carry – your plan
- Convey – through action

Let's take a closer look.

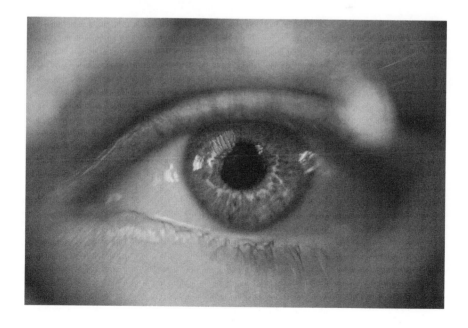

Catch Your Vision

The first thing you need to do is to completely understand what it is you are working towards. What is it that you want to achieve? When do you want to achieve it by? How will you know you have been successful?

When you try to visualise what you want, and to see your future self with your dreams made reality, different images can flit around your brain like butterflies; you need to catch them and pin them down, so that you know exactly what success looks like. Catch your vision.

<u>Carry Your Plan</u>

If you look at the gap between where you are now and where you want to be, it can seem like far too big a step for you to take. And it would be, if you were to try to make it all happen in just one leap!

The way to make a dream into a reality is to have a plan.

Break the big leaps down into achievable steps. Make a note of the people you think could help you and the resources you'll need to get things done. Add some deadlines, so you can be sure you keep moving forward at a reasonable rate.

Once you have your plan prepared, get ready to take that first step. And carry that plan with you – remember, it's the route map for the journey you're on.

Convey Through Action

Every time you take another step and reach another deadline on your plan, you are conveying yourself closer to your vision through the power of your actions.

Stay focused: keep your eyes on the prize.

When it comes to your vision, be unwavering in your determination. When it comes to your plan, accept that you might need to be flexible, so you can get around any obstacles you meet along the way.

If you were driving home for a big family occasion and the road you planned to take was blocked, you wouldn't try to force your way through, somehow – it would be a waste of effort. Neither would you sit and wait for the road to reopen – it would be a waste of time and you might miss the big event.

The sensible thing to do is to find a way round.

You end up at the same place at the same time (give or take), despite your very sensible detour.

Chapter 3
Blueprint To Bring Out The Best In You

"You must expect great things of yourself before you can do them." Michael Jordan

If you want to achieve something out of the ordinary, to make your mark, make waves and make history, you have to be your very best self, operating at your highest level of ability.

In order to be able to do that, you have to understand what you want to achieve and what success will look and feel like. You have to understand how to get from where you are now to where you want to be. You have to appreciate that on the journey, you will encounter boosters and obstacles, and to know how you will deal with them. Most importantly, and underpinning everything else, you have to understand yourself.

The underlying message of this book is that you are fine as you are, imperfections included, and that you really should stop doubting yourself and go after what you want, with gusto. You are good enough. You can do this. Believe in yourself.

Make This Your Mantra:

I Am Good Enough.

I Can Do This.

I Believe In Myself.

I believe we all have an inner "best" that's an inherent part of who and how we are. If you are going to achieve your dreams, you need to dig deep and find that best version of you.

To help you to do that, I'd like to share with you, in the following chapters, what I believe are the eleven essential strategies that, together, form a blueprint that will allow you to bring out the best in you, in every situation.

Blueprint to bring out the best in you

Get to know yourself
- Understand your motivation
- Identify your inspiration

Set yourself up to succeed
- Plan for success
- Realise your inner ability
- See the ability in every disability

Step into your power
- Be unstoppable
- Let go of insecurities
- Believe that everything is possible
- Get unstuck

Be bold and embrace your dream

- Live a life without limits
- Reinvent your future with the power of transformation

Stick to this formula and it will, inevitably, lead you to the success you so desire – and so richly deserve.

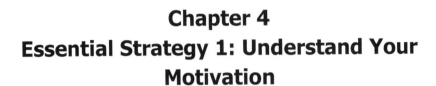

Chapter 4
Essential Strategy 1: Understand Your Motivation

Motivation is what keeps you going. Your motivation is your "why" and it's important to understand what yours is – when times get rough, it's the thing that fuels you to keep driving forward towards your next goal.

Take some time to list the things that motivate you and make you feel like you want to keep going.

What Is Demotivation?

Demotivation is the other side of the coin. It's equally important to understand what makes you feel like giving up, so that you can avoid those things and not be affected by their destructive nature.

Learn to recognise what saps your energy and drive, then take steps to avoid those things.

If you are affected by them, go to your "motivation" list and use something that fuels your desire to succeed to kick-start your journey again.

Keys To Motivating Yourself:

- **Identify The Areas You Want To Improve**

Identify what your strengths and weaknesses are. You need to play to your strengths and work on your weaknesses. The aim is to turn your weaknesses into strengths.

For example, you are going to have to be confident when it comes to approaching other people. How do you feel about that?

Personally, I have always enjoyed talking to people. I've always enjoyed developing friendships with strangers. For me, it's a strength. How about you? Is it something you are adept at, or something you have to work on?

Identify those areas that are likely to need some work to improve your abilities and skills. Without a good understanding of yourself, it is undeniably difficult to either improve, or to effectively respond to others.

• Start Small

Do the things that you enjoy doing and that will move you closer towards your vision, to get some easy, early gains. It doesn't have to be a big dramatic gesture – just make a start. Don't be afraid to take that first step forward.

It is said that: "Great things in life come from small beginnings." Well, that's true. It applies not just to some, but to everyone.

• Don't Procrastinate

To procrastinate means to delay or postpone something – to think, *I'll start tomorrow.*

Procrastination is a centuries-old trap that people have often fallen into. It's an active process and is different from laziness.

You need to identify and understand the reason for your procrastination – whether that is fear, feeling overwhelmed or something else – before you tackle it.

The best quality result comes from a job done well and without procrastination. Get it done. Instead of saying you are starting tomorrow, commit to making a start today.

• Take Tiny Steps In The Right Direction

When I discovered I was able to catch the attention of people when I spoke, I started addressing small crowds.

And that's a great strategy: start small – do what you enjoy doing on a reduced scale, first, and become confident in your ability to do it well.

Then, when you have mastered that, start envisioning yourself speaking to a bigger crowd.

I began small then, in my mind, I began picturing myself speaking in front of a thousand people. And yes, it happened right before my eyes.

If I hadn't first spoken to that small crowd, I wouldn't be who I am today: a motivational speaker comfortable in front of a much bigger audience.

If you put your mind to it – and put it to your mind, by envisioning success – you'll be surprised at what you can achieve.

• **Reduce Daily Distractions**

Be focused. Know what you want and don't get distracted by noise. Switch off your music, get away from Instagram and Facebook – understand your distractions, stay in your zone of focus, and do what you have to do. There'll be time to have fun afterwards, and you'll enjoy it all the more because you won't feel guilty that you didn't do the work, first!

Your
INNER
PEACE
Matters.

• Be Accountable

Make sure to get a mentor or a coach who can check you and hold you accountable. It's necessary nowadays to have someone who would remind you of the things you should be focusing on, if you suddenly get distracted. Your mentor or coach will get you back on track to keep your eye on your goal.

• Be Optimistic

Don't ever write yourself off, because the moment you do that, you have accepted that you aren't good enough. And you are!

Remember: you are good enough; you can do this; believe in yourself.

Always keep your main vision in mind, believe it's achievable, and go ahead and make it happen.

LOVE
And
KINDNESS
Are The Gifts To
Heal Humanity.

- **Be Kind To Yourself When You Stumble Or Make Mistakes**

Because of my disability, I can be clumsy. I used to feel useless every time I broke an egg or a glass. It took me a while to stop feeling like that. Please don't make the same mistake.

Accept that errors and accidents do happen and, when they do, it's just a part of the learning process. Try not to dwell on your mistakes, but instead put your efforts into working out how you can improve.

- ## Only Compare Yourself To Yourself

A lot of people compare themselves to others. You should never compare yourself to other people – you are in competition only with yourself. If you can see the improvement in yourself, then you are heading in the right direction.

"Always dream and shoot higher than you know you can do. Don't bother just to be better than your contemporaries or predecessors. Try to be better than yourself." William Faulkner

Always remember – you are not in competition with anyone but yourself.

- **Remind Yourself Why You Are Working Towards Your Dreams**

It's important to remember why you want your vision to become a reality, as that means you will be more likely to achieve it. It may be a personal thing, but remember that your vision also incorporates your environment, and so includes the significant people in your life.

It is extremely easy to lose motivation when you get disconnected from your purpose in life. Always remind yourself why you chose this path you are on right now and stay focused on your goal.

• Be Grateful For What You've Got

If you aren't grateful, it closes the door for more to come into your life. Gratefulness opens more doors of opportunity for you.

If you are grateful, people will want to help you more.

If you are grateful, good things will flow in your life without you fighting and striving to get them. Things come naturally. Remember, positive attracts positive.

- ## Adjust Your Goal Size

If you don't adjust your goal size, you become stagnant.

When I was thinking of writing a book, all I envisioned was holding the published book in my hands. That was enough in itself. Then I learnt that there were several ways to turn a book into additional streams of income, for example, by turning it into a course.

And now, I have finally published my own book, and not only am I proud of what I have achieved, I also understand how to leverage it to provide additional income streams – and to help more people.

You should also seek out ways in which you can maximise your goal to achieve your vision. Be creative and do not limit your imagination. It will take you to ideas and places you never thought you'd go to.

- **Reward Yourself And Celebrate Your Success**

Too often, we're very good at beating ourselves up about things that don't go right, but we forget to celebrate the things that do go right.

If you have a success, celebrate it. Treat yourself to something you enjoy.

I enjoy eating well, and I like to invite my friends to join me. If you are a people person, celebrate with your family and friends. If not, then treat yourself by buying something you really want or doing something that will bring joy to you.

★ ⭐ ★

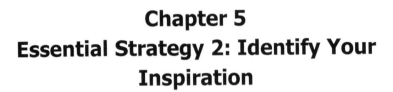

Chapter 5
Essential Strategy 2: Identify Your Inspiration

Inspiration is subjective – the things that inspire you might not be an inspiration to others.

You'll get the most powerful inspiration from people who are like you, or who are pursuing a similar dream. Those are the people you'll be able to relate to most closely.

How Do You Get Inspired?

- ## Listen To Inspirational Talks

Many motivational speakers have moving backstories that inspire others. It can help to give you a different perspective on life. You can get inspired by them and how, despite the adversities they faced, they achieved their dreams. That will help you to believe you can achieve your own dreams. Listening to inspirational speakers from various fields will augment your ideas and boost your knowledge on certain topics. Plus, it will help you keep updated on the latest trends.

- ## Learn From Your Role Models

Identify those people who are considered to be role models in your chosen field. You can learn from them both directly and indirectly.

Direct learning takes place when you are able to ask them how they carried out the plans that helped them reach the level they are at right now. That might be face-to-face at an event or a talk.

Indirect learning takes place through active observation, such as watching YouTube videos or following their news.

You can use social media for both direct and indirect learning, by following and interacting with your role models.

Innovate, based on your observation and learning. Get what you can from it and reflect on whether their approach suits you, too.

Stay realistic about your capacity for action at any one time, but do take action. A wonderful result surely awaits you. Gather your courage ... just take that first single step and you'll see your life begin to change.

- ## Write Down What You Want In Your Life

Writing down what you want in life is a great idea. Seeing those things on paper – or on a screen – makes your dreams appear to be both tangible and achievable. Also, if you are having a rough day and wondering why you are putting yourself through this, that list will act as a terrific source of both inspiration and motivation.

However, I worry that a lot of people fall into the trap of quantity-based engagement. That's the trap of believing that you need to make it BIG and have A LOT of material things in life in order to be considered successful – the fancy car, huge house and jet-set lifestyle.

You don't; you can start small. Write down the things that you want, ranking first the smaller things that are easier to achieve, then the bigger things, that take more effort. Take it one step at a time. Start with small gains and easy wins. Every single one is another step on your journey.

FIGHT
For What You Want.

• Create A Plan Of Action And A Strategy For Accomplishing It

If there's something you want to do, you need to give yourself opportunities to be able to do it. Go to where people are learning and talking about it, and actively participating in it. If you want to be a performance poet, for example, get along to some local events. If there's an open slot, get up and do your stuff. When you have more confidence, maybe look for a poetry slam.

I attended a few speaker seminars to understand the concept of speaking and get to grips with what the speaking business actually means. I started small, then sought out a bigger audience. If you are gifted in this field, don't wait for invitations to come to you. You need to plan a good strategy and actively seek out speaking opportunities.

- **Take Action**

Once you understand what inspires you, start putting your plan into action. Take each item on your agenda in turn and get them done. It takes courage, hard work and determination to materialise your passion – but it all starts with just one step. You don't need to do what you're doing for a lot of people, you can start with just one or a few. You may not be able to change the world for everyone, but you can always change their world for someone.

- **Accomplish Your Goals**

Goal setting is a process – things don't just happen the way you want them to because that's what you want. You can't simply say, "I want this", I will get that", and expect things to fall into your lap. That's passively wishing for something, not actively pursuing a goal.

To accomplish your goals takes time and a lot of effort. You should be mindful of the process, because that's where you get significant learning. Remember: it's not the result that teaches us, but the process.

★

---- ⋆ ★ ⋆ ----

Chapter 6
Essential Strategy 3: Plan For Success

First, you need to define what success means to you, then you need to develop a plan to allow you to achieve it.

If you don't understand what success means to you, on your own terms, you can end up valuing the wrong things and not appreciating the right ones. It's an important process; your level of contentment depends on it.

If you don't have a plan, you don't have a chance. Planning turns dreams into realities.

Develop A Plan To Achieve What You Want:

- **Take Action To Accomplish It**

Developing your plan is important, but then you need to take action. Once you begin to take action, you can feel like you have already begun to succeed.

If you try something that doesn't work out, you can learn from that and try again.

Henry Ford said: "Failure is simply the opportunity to begin again, this time more intelligently."

Use failure as a source of inspiration.

★ ⭐ ★

Channel Your Energy Into Today.

Yesterday Is Gone.

• Giving Up Isn't An Option In Pursuit Of Success

Find a way through your failure, so you get to success. Don't count your failures, count the number of times you stand up and try again, because that's what matters.

There's an old proverb that goes: "If at first you don't succeed, try, try again."

You aren't defined by your lack of success, you are defined by the amount of courage you show every time you stand up and try again.

• **Work Hard – And Work Smart**

Yes, it's important to work hard, but you'll get more bang for your buck if you also work smart.

Here are my six essential tips for working smarter:

1. Do the things that are important and urgent first.
2. Do one thing at a time.
3. Finish what you start.
4. Avoid distractions.
5. Know the value of your time and don't waste it.
6. Use technology to help you, where you can.

Yes, you have to work hard to make success happen, but working smarter can turbo boost the results of your hard work.

No One Is Going To Give You An Easy Ride

To Stand Up Take The Ride And Be Counted

Chapter 7
Essential Strategy 4: Realise Your Inner Ability

Identify what it is that you are truly and passionately interested in. Focus on those things you both love and are good at. Are you good with words? Are you good with your hands? Are you an inspirational speaker?

If you aren't sure what your greatest strength and ability is, ask a trusted friend; they'll tell you the truth, from a standpoint of love.

Do What You Enjoy:

Talking to people, interacting, playing tennis, acting ... tap into whatever brings you joy.

I enjoy having a conversation with someone. It's my niche in the market. Apart from talking, I also enjoy playing tennis and football.

I schedule free time into my diary to help balance my life. Make sure you schedule free time in your diary, too – your life shouldn't just revolve around work. You need some work/life balance.

Create time for yourself, so you can take your kids to visit your family, spend time with them and do what you enjoy doing.

Taking some time off will help you stay sane in the midst of your busy schedule. Life is better when it's balanced. A healthy life means a well-balanced life.

Realise You Have An Ability:

Everyone has a special gift. My gift is definitely different from yours.

We are not aware of how great we are until we discover what we're capable of. When we don't feel we are smart, beautiful, talented, we sometimes lose our self-confidence.

Personally, I believe that God has given us unique gifts so that we may be of help to others.

"Stop acting so small. You are the universe in ecstatic motion." Rumi, 13th-century Persian poet, jurist, Islamic scholar and theologian.

You must discover your gift. Here are some ways that can help you find it.

Your Gift Will Make Room For You,

WORK YOUR GIFT.

• Ask People Around You

More often than not, it's the people around you who will become aware of your capabilities first. Why?

Because sometimes you don't see them for yourself. You are too focused on the idea of "others", what others are good at and capable of, and so you don't spot that there are areas in which you also excel.

Now, ask your friends, family, relatives or mentors what they think your talents or gifts are. Listen with an open mind, and don't dismiss anything in haste, because you think they are flattering you.

Remember, we are the people often least able to see our own strengths. They can see what we cannot.

- **Check Your Gift Within Your Adversity**

What do you usually do during tough times? How do you overcome challenges?

Take note of these behaviours; they are also gifts that you possess.

You can help others by sharing your coping strategies – they might work for them, too.

Develop That Ability:

Find a course to help you develop your ability. I focus on communication courses, so I can be a better communicator.

Self-development takes time and effort, and often money, too, and not everyone is prepared to invest in it. It depends on how hungry you are.

Go To Free Events And Learn:

Free events are great, and can very much be a win–win situation.

Not only can you learn from the speaker, you can also give them feedback, if that's appropriate.

It's a good idea to get some thoughts down soon after the event – what worked and what didn't; what you could perhaps also do and what wouldn't suit your own personal style.

I have attended a lot of events where I've learned a lot about public speaking, and have also offered unbiased and fair feedback, when asked.

Pick Up All The Right Information:

You need to gather information that will first benefit you, and then benefit other people. This is information or knowledge that you gain and can then share, that will inspire others to take action in their lives.

Write A Book About Your Topic:

Become an authority in a particular area. Don't try to be all things to all people, but specialise.

When you are an authority, people will listen to you more. A book is also something people can read over and over again, when they are in need of inspiration in their everyday lives.

Your book is part of your legacy, it is something you will leave behind to be remembered by.

Sell Your Products And Make Money:

Selling your products is another way of generating an income. Not only will you be able to help other people solve their problems as a result of them buying your products, but you will also be helping yourself, by using those sales as a way to earn a living.

Overcome Disability:

I never thought of becoming a speaker until I did a short interview with my boss at work – it was an eye-opener. I was getting great feedback and I realised it was an opportunity for me to create something for myself.

I then started looking at how to improve my speaking ability, and as a result, I met a lot of interesting people.

You will find the same to be true, if you make an effort to overcome adversity, in whatever form you are currently coping with it. You might be terribly shy, or have restricted mobility, or struggle with language. Whatever it is, I urge you to try to overcome it. If I, who had a speech impediment, can become a motivational speaker then you, too, can overcome disability and achieve success.

I am now exploring writing more books. I believe if I can channel my disability as a differentiator in the market, I can serve as many people as possible. I take it one day at a time.

★

Chapter 8
Essential Strategy 5: See The Ability In Every Disability

The universe didn't create anybody without a purpose. The fact that you are here means that you are here to *do something*.

Whether you have a disability or not, you must find out what your purpose is and achieve it.

Everyone has their own unique purpose in life – don't let any disability or disadvantage stop you from achieving your full potential. Disability is a matter of perception.

─────────────── ⋆ ★ ⋆ ───────────────

Never Let Anyone Place A Limit On Your Ability.

Only You Should Be Allowed To

DETERMINE YOUR LIMIT.

─────────────── ⋆ ★ ⋆ ───────────────

What Disability Is:

If you don't know what it is, you are likely to abuse it. I was a late developer in some ways, because of cerebral palsy. For example, I couldn't take a bath by myself until I was ten. I couldn't do a lot of things that others take for granted until I was older, and I had to try harder to be able to do them, but these are the experiences that got me to where I am right now.

I am always improving every day. Because I keep learning and expanding my knowledge, skills and abilities, I feel like I don't have a disability anymore.

And always remember: disability doesn't mean "inability", it means "differently able".

Look For Ways To Turn Your Disability Into An Ability:

I was told I wouldn't be able to speak clearly, so I went to speech therapy.

I was dropping a lot of things out of my hands, so I went to a physiotherapist to help me with that.

I struggled to swallow, and so had too much saliva in my mouth, and I got help with that, too.

All of this has helped me to become the person I am today, but if there's one thing that I overcame that stands out for me, it was improving my ability to talk. Once I was better able to communicate, there wasn't a happier person than me. No wonder I revel in motivational speaking!

- **Overcome Adversity**

How you seek to overcome adversity depends on the form it takes.

If you have financial adversity, see a financial adviser and borrow books on financial education from the library.

If you and your partner are suffering from emotional adversity, get a relationship coach.

If you can't have a baby, you need to see a doctor.

There's help out there, no matter what adversity you face. It can take courage to admit there's a problem, but that's the hardest step. Everything after that is about helping you to overcome whatever it is that is adversely affecting you.

• **Use Your Disability To Your Advantage**

You can use your disability to get a lot of help and assistance. For example, if you apply for a job, they will guarantee an interview to any disabled person.

You can get a free bus pass to take you around London.

The NHS provides a range of free walking aids, from sticks to wheelchairs to mobility scooters.

Make sure you take advantage of whatever is on offer; it's all intended to help make your life easier.

Chapter 9
Essential Strategy 6: Be Unstoppable

What It Means To Be Unstoppable:

No matter how many times you fail, you can always pick yourself back up and try again. Failure isn't an option, and failure isn't a barrier you can't overcome; it is a stepping stone to success. Always believe in yourself, and you will be unstoppable.

Limitations You Have Today Are The Stepping Stones To The

NEXT LEVEL.

- **Don't Take No For An Answer**

If someone says what you want to do isn't achievable, find a way to make it achievable – even if it means you need to work twice as hard.

Remember, not everyone has your best interests at heart. Some people might want to stop you from achieving your dream because they are jealous, others because they don't want things to change.

However, you are unstoppable, because you have no limit to where you can get in your mind if you work harder and smarter.

● **Work Hard To Achieve Your Success – Whatever Success Means To You**

We all have our own definition of success. I have my definition, my friend has her own, and so has everyone else.

What's yours? You need to define success in your life. When your success is clearly defined, that's when the magic begins.

- **Keep Working Hard**

There is no room for slacking off when you're in this game called life. Hard work pays off in the form of good results.

- ## Keep Working Smart

Keep your focus on what you want to achieve.

Understand your strongest areas and further develop them. Be aware of your weaknesses – procrastination, distraction, starting things but not getting them finished – and work on them so they don't hold you back.

Release Your
GREATNESS.

• Find A Way Where There Isn't One

"Where there's a will, there's a way." Sounds like a cliché, doesn't it? But there's always truth behind this phrase.

Your "will" is a key that can open doors of opportunity. It has the ability to unlock impossible paths.

If you are sufficiently determined, you will succeed.

• Develop Your Ability To Navigate Difficult Situations

Being able to navigate through life is a gift, a gift that we all have. Some people struggle to find their true path, but it's innate in each one of us.

I have this ability and so do you; we just have to follow our instincts.

★ ⭐ ★

LIFE IS TOUGH,
But To Make It To
The End,
You Must
DEVELOP
CHARACTER.

Chapter 10
Essential Strategy 7: Let Go Of Insecurities

Discover What Your Insecurities Are:

I have always been insecure because of my disability. I developed my abilities by reading books and attending various seminars. I went to see the GP a lot, to get the help I needed to improve, physically. I saw a psychologist to help me to get rid of the baggage I was carrying, mentally. It was weighing me down, I didn't need it.

I had anger issues when I was growing up, because of my disability. I had a lot of self-doubt. I genuinely thought I could not achieve anything.

Then I began to listen to motivational tapes by people including Les Brown. I really enjoy Joel Osteen, as well. I try and pick up valuable lessons from people like them and I say to myself, "It is possible to live the life I want to live."

And it is – I know, because I am living it.

BE CAREFUL WHO YOU TRUST

Most Likely They Are The One Who Will Betray You.

Surround Yourself With Achievers Or Role Models Who Have Gone Through This Situation Before, And Use Them As A Guide To Get Rid Of Insecurities:

I don't hang out with people that have gone through the same situation as me, but I do talk about it with people I trust. For example, I spoke to my mother and uncle, and other members of my family, including my sister and my brother.

I listened to my late father, when I was younger. His name is Olujimi Asuni, and he was a wise man.

I listened to what motivational speakers said – Les Brown – Joel Osteen – Myles Munroe – John Maxwell.

I listened to gospel singer Muyiwa Olarewaju and Tasha Cobbs

You might not be able to get rid of your insecurities, but you can manage them.

Les Brown says that to achieve anything worthwhile, you have to be hungry.

I implemented some of their ideas in my life. I write down a lot of my visions, so I can see them when I wake up. I also read and write a lot.

I made the decision that every time I am in my house, even if I'm not planning to go out, I would present myself in a particular way. That way, if I need to go out unexpectedly, I'm ready; I don't go anywhere wearing a dirty T-shirt, for example.

You must know how to talk, where to talk, and what to say. You must seize any opportunity you are offered to improve yourself.

I used to work and go along with the flow of the day, but I now plan my day. I say my prayers, then I bathe, then I work, then I come back home. This has taught me to manage and prioritise my time.

ENVY
And
JEALOUSY
Is What Keeps The
World In A
Dark Place.

You Must Be Hungry To Overcome Your Insecurities:

If you aren't hungry, you can't achieve anything.

You must be able to go out and do what you want to do. If you stay at home when you don't have a job, then it's hard to break the cycle of inertia and achieve what you want.

Feel the hunger. Get passionate about your goal. Then get out and do something!

Overcome Your Insecurities:

I don't think you can totally get rid of your insecurities, but once you have overcome them to the point they no longer hold you back, you will become a better person.

I Made It This Far, Because

I NEVER GAVE UP

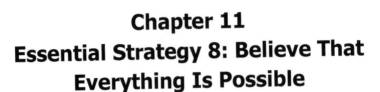

Chapter 11
Essential Strategy 8: Believe That Everything Is Possible

What Possibilities Are:

A possibility is a thing that may happen; equally, it may not. The outcome is often up to you alone.

- **Possibilities Exist Only In Your Mind**

Henry Ford said, "Whether you think you can or you think you can't, you're right."

I was determined to show people I had a great skill as an orator, so I did a lot of studying, and a lot of self-improvement, and I went to speech therapy to improve my speech.

My dream went from being a possibility that existed only in my mind to becoming a reality, because I had a vision and I worked towards it one step at a time.

Let Go Of Negativity, EMBRACE POSITIVITY

- **Believe In Your Heart Everything Is Possible**

The mind is a very powerful tool. Whatever you focus your attention on, you draw to yourself. Like attracts like – so positive attracts positive.

Believe that, if you want something badly enough, even though it might take you some time to achieve it, you will get it, eventually.

You Are A Product Of Your
THOUGHT

- ## Identify Key Areas That Can Help You Move From Impossibility To Possibility

In my case, as well as focusing on self-improvement, I sought help from specialists to help me overcome certain issues I faced due to my disability.

Where could you do with some help or improvement? What one thing would be a big boost when it comes to making your dream a reality?

Always be alert to any opportunity that can help you move closer to where you want to be. If someone offers an opportunity, take it, and learn as you go along – even if you feel you aren't yet prepared.

Remember: if you can see it in your mind's eye, if you can believe it in your heart, you can receive it in your reality.

★

———— ⋆ ★ ⋆ ————

Chapter 12
Essential Strategy 9: Get Unstuck

First, Realise That You Are Stuck:

When you keep going round and round in circles in your life, that means you are stuck. If the same issues are coming up again and again, you have stopped moving forward and must take some action to first, identify the issue, then break out of the pattern of repetition.

- **Identify Why You Are Stuck**

You need to identify what's stopping you. Whatever the issue, you need to analyse, reflect and recognise it for what it is. Only when you fully understand the reason for the blockage will you be able to take steps to deal with it and move on again.

There are arguably three major reasons why you get stuck:

1. Fear.
2. Limiting beliefs.
3. Past experiences.

Let's take a closer look.

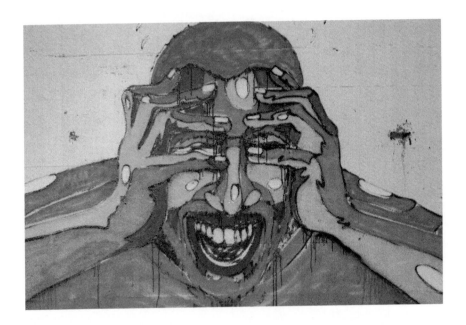

Fear

Fear is a major reason why people get stuck. One of the biggest fears people experience is fear of change. Even someone in a situation they hate – a rotten job or a bad relationship, for example – will stay where they are because they think, *better the devil you know* ...

Have you reached a critical moment, and is fear of the big change you are about to trigger preventing you from acting? Is the next step on your plan too big, and so you are afraid to make that leap?

Limiting Beliefs

Whatever you believe to be true becomes your reality. If you don't think you can take things to the next level, then you can't. If you don't think you'll ever master a particular skill, then you won't

In the words of Les Brown: "Life has no limitations, except the ones you make."

Past Experiences

If you've tried to do something in the past and failed, it's easier to walk away than to pick yourself up and try again. But unless you do pick yourself up and try again, you'll never be able to move on and fulfill your potential.

- **Discover Ways To Become Unstuck, Depending On The Reason For It**

The way in which you get unstuck will depend on the reason for becoming stuck in the first place. Having said that, the one common denominator for all of these issues is that you will need courage, determination and commitment.

If your problem is fear ...

You need to get beyond fear. There are always going to be new situations, things to do for the first time and new skills and abilities to be mastered. Unless you want to stay in the confines of a small comfort zone, fear is going to be a regular companion on your journey.

Take steps to deal with the fear, either through coaching or self-study. Also, make sure you reward yourself when you overcome a fear and move past it. Rituals like this can be really helpful in the process of making your dreams a reality.

If your problem is limiting beliefs ...

A life coach, if you can afford one, is a great way to investigate, uncover and conquer limiting beliefs. If not, then look for relevant self-help books or even YouTube videos. But aim to get out of that rut and stop listening to the inner voice that is trying to keep you small.

If your problem is past experiences ...

Throughout our lives, we learn to tell ourselves stories – but these stories are very often not true. So, you didn't succeed at your first attempt ... so what? Not everyone passes their driving test first time round; that doesn't mean they should abandon their dream completely!

It can be hard, I know, but pick yourself up and try again. As a first step, you could go back to your plan and see if it's the plan that's flawed. Maybe the step is too big. Maybe it's a misstep, and you need to redefine it. Once you are confident your plan is right, there is no reason not to give it another go.

Develop A Plan To Get Yourself Unstuck

Once you know what you're dealing with, you can develop a plan to overcome the issue. Use the information above to help you.

If the old feelings threaten to surface, use your mantra: I am good enough; I can do this; I believe in myself.

Take Action On Your Plan

This is just the same as taking action on your main plan, the one that is guiding you on your journey to making your dreams a reality. Take it one step at a time. Get into the habit of taking regular actions. Don't stop now – you've done the hardest bit!

You Are Definitely On The Right Path

You'll know you're on the right path when you start seeing and experiencing new things, rather than going around in circles. This stage will feel really good – you'll experience a sense of freedom and lightness that keeps you moving forward.

Take The Limit Off.
YOU CAN DO IT

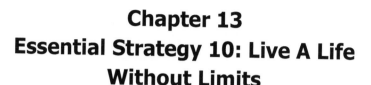

Chapter 13
Essential Strategy 10: Live A Life Without Limits

Your Attitude Is What Limits You:

If you look up "attitude" in the Oxford English Dictionary, you will see the following definition:

A settled way of thinking or feeling about something.

If your attitude is that you cannot do it, you won't do it. If you think you can do it, then you will do it.

Your

ATTITUDE

Is A Product Of Your

BELIEF

Your Mind Is What Limits You:

You have to see things in your mind before you can manifest them. That can be something tangible, like a car, or intangible, like self-confidence and self-esteem. It must come from the invisible.

I saw in my mind that I was going to write a book. I didn't know how I was going to achieve it but I knew I was going to do it, because I wanted to share my experience with others, who would benefit from it.

Then, I met the people who helped me put it together.

Your mind is a powerful tool. Whatever you tell your mind, you accomplish.

Expand Your Mind:

Feed your mind with good thoughts. Read good books that can help expand your knowledge and understanding. The more information you have and the better you can apply it, the more your mind expands. That will help you expand your thinking.

We all learn from other people, either through talking with them, watching videos of them or reading what they have written. I read a lot of ideas, and I embrace the ones that resonate with me and help me to expand my mind.

If You Can
SEE
It In Your Mind,
You Can
HAVE
It In Your Hand.

Live An Abundant Life:

It all starts in the mind. If you expand your mind, you will live an extraordinary life.

Don't keep yourself small – remember that you deserve success.

Find mentors and learn from them. Join a mastermind group. Keep up your learning, whether that's formal or informal.

Don't tell yourself you can't – use your mantra instead ... because you *are* good enough, and you *can* do this, and you *should* believe in yourself.

You Don't Attract What You Want, But

WHO YOU ARE

Change Your Circle Of Friends:

If you don't change your circle of friends, your mind doesn't get expanded.

If you don't change your circle of friends, you cannot reflect who you want to be and how you want to feel. Other people's energy is contagious. Surround yourself with people who are striving for the same things you are, and who are at roughly the same stage of the journey. Don't hang out with people who will drag you down and hold you back.

If you show me five of your closest friends, I will tell you where you are going, because you are the product of the five people you are in touch with constantly. Make sure that where you are going is somewhere worth arriving at.

★ ⭐ ★

Whenever A Great Shift Is About To Happen,
It Is Always Through The
INTRODUCTION Of A Person Or A RELATIONSHIP.

★ ⭐ ★

* ★ *

Chapter 14
Essential Strategy 11: Reinvent Your Future With The Power Of Transformation

Define What Transformation Is:

According to the Oxford English Dictionary, "transformation" is:

"A marked change in form, nature, or appearance."

You need to change yourself, if you are to step into your power and achieve your dream. The current you can't make that step.

You'll need to transform your thinking, your outlook and your mindset, for a start, so you can begin to become the person you envision when you see yourself with your dreams fulfilled.

You have to be willing to change, and to embrace the new you wholeheartedly. If you keep on doing the same things in the same way, you will always get the same results. Grab every opportunity that will allow you to further metamorphose into the person you know you were born to be.

Be The

CHANGE

You Wish To See In The World

What Kind Of Future Do You See For Yourself?:

I see a future where I'm giving motivational talks based on my book in front of thousands of people, all around the world – that is where I am headed.

What about you? What does your future look like?

Once you know, you need to identify a place where you are able to learn from people that are doing this already.

Transform Your Mind And Achieve Anything:

Everything is in your mind. Everything begins with a thought, that becomes a desire, then a belief.

You can change the way you think, which will allow you to totally transform your life. Turn negative thoughts into positive thoughts to attract more positivity into your life.

I have grown and improved myself as a person, and so can you.

THINK, ACT

And

SEE

Yourself As You Want To Be, Not As You Now

Know Where You Are Currently:

Make an honest assessment of where you currently are. This will be your starting point.

Understand Where You Need To Be:

Have a clear vision of where you need to be. If you don't know where you want to end up, how will know what you need to do to get there? And how can you possibly know when you've arrived?

Once I realised where I wanted to be was in a position to start using my life as a way of inspiring people, I was able to start planning to get there.

Understand What You Need To Do To Accomplish Your Transformation Goals:

Armed with the knowledge of where you are now and where you want to be, you can develop a plan that helps you bridge the gap. You have to be prepared to do whatever it takes to end up exactly where you need and want to be.

Reinvent Yourself:

Change always starts with you.

If nothing is working out, it's time to reinvent yourself. By reinventing yourself, you will be able to change your life.

Learn About What You Want To Achieve Through:

- Online sources, such as relevant websites and YouTube.
- Magazines.
- Training courses.
- Workshops.

It's best to learn using a variety of different methods and teachers – that way, you get to see things from different viewpoints.

Get A Transformation Coach Or Mentor:

If you can afford it, working one-to-one with a transformation coach can be life-changing. It can affect everything, from how you think, to how you see yourself, to how others perceive you.

Another great thing to do is to try to get taken on by a mentor. Learning from someone who is much more advanced and experienced can help you to grow and develop more quickly – and stop you from making mistakes!

A further option is to join a mastermind group. These are peer-to-peer problem-solving groups that can really help with some tricky issues. Because they're peer-to-peer, there will come a time when you have to move on to a different group operating at a higher level. This regular change of group members helps keep things fresh.

★

Chapter 15
Find Something You Are Passionate About

You are planning to embark on your life journey, to head towards your dream future, to commit to it wholeheartedly. That being the case, you really need to find something you like doing, because you're going to be doing a lot of it!

Write a list of things you enjoy and are good at, then try and whittle it down to the one you enjoy the most. If it helps, choose a top three, then list the pros and cons of each, to help you make your final decision.

Once you find the one you enjoy the most, identify people that have already started down that route and reach out to them. Ask them to be your mentor, and to share with you the success they had – then follow the steps they took.

1. Invest In Finding Out More About Your Passion

When I discovered I could talk to people, I decided to look for free speaking engagements that I could do. That allowed me to make connections with people and to share my passion. If people like what they hear, they buy into what you are talking about.

If you find the right people – people that can help you push your dream forward – then reach out to them and ask them for help.

Book an appointment to see them, to show you are serious about what you want to achieve – then they will take time from their business schedule to help you achieve your dreams.

Because I reached out to people, they are taking the time to help me reach my goals.

2.   Turn Your Passion To Financial Gain

There are many ways you can turn your passion to financial gain, including e-books, print books, and turning your book into a workshop

You can become a life coach by creating a step-by-step programme people can follow to achieve their goals.

Share information about your book when it's published – market your book everywhere.

Realise you need to brand yourself – building a brand is key to your success. You need to know how you come across in your book, so you can brand yourself appropriately. Read books and blogs, watch videos, and learn how to do it.

LEARNING
Requires ENERGY

3. <u>Find Out Who Already Achieved Your Passion, Ask Them Questions, So You Can Get The Same Results, Aim To Learn The Steps They Took</u>

You'd be surprised how willing people can be to help others. It's always worth reaching out – after all, the worst thing that can happen is that they say no!

Overcome Adversity:

You need to face the adversities you have in life head on, then take steps to overcome them, in order to be successful. Adversities are opportunities in disguise. It will help build your character.

Chapter 16
Goal-Setting And Getting What You Want

1. Have A Clear Idea In Your Mind Of What You Want, Specifically

We talked earlier about Catch, Carry, Convey. This relates to the "catch" stage.

As well as writing down how you want your future life to look, it's a great idea to create a vision board. You can do this on computer, with text and a series of images you find online, or physically, using an actual board, and words and images you cut out of magazines.

It's a great idea to include your mantra:

I Am Good Enough.
I Can Do This.
I Believe In Myself.

Look at your vision board regularly and, if your vision for the future changes or becomes more refined, you can either update it or start afresh and make a new one that better reflects who you are now and what you're working towards.

2. Set Goals That Will Make Your Vision A Reality

Break down your overall goal into smaller steps, and add dates for when milestones will be reached. Keep track of your progress.

If you fail to meet a milestone, go back to the plan and review it. Is the plan flawed, or have you been lazy? Get back on track as soon as you can.

⋆ ★ ⋆

Dress The Way You Want To Be ADDRESSED

* ★ *

Chapter 17
The Way You Show Yourself Makes You Different

1. How Do You See Yourself?

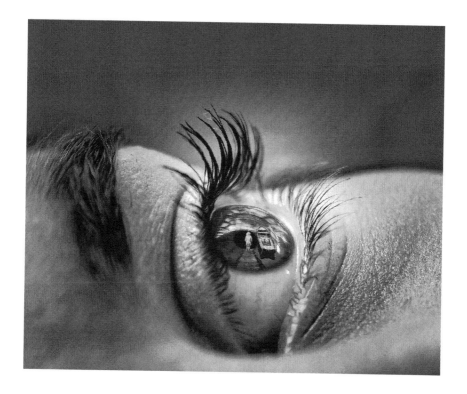

I see myself as a speaker already – I present myself like a speaker.

I used to see myself speaking to people and I had a vision in my head. I remember standing in front of my mirror and presenting, as if I were presenting to people – I was imagining it in my mind, I was looking at myself in the mirror, and I was presenting as if I was talking to people.

That's how I was envisioning myself.

I would record my voice as I was speaking and I would play it back to myself. I was practicing. Practice makes you perfect. If you want something, you have to practice until you master it.

When the opportunity came, I was ready for it.

I am not surprised I am writing a book, as this is also something I have practiced behind closed doors.

You need to practice multiple times. Say you want to learn how to swim – you can't just jump in the water and suddenly you can do it. It takes practice. This applies to running, too, for example, if you want to increase your speed. Usain Bolt practiced for years before he became an Olympic champion.

If you fail, get up and try again. Keep trying. Failure isn't an option.

The first time you do something is always nerve-racking. You're bound to feel fear. But if you have the courage to try, and you continue to practice, you should achieve what you were meant to achieve.

Your personality must shine through. That's what people will relate to.

2. **How Do Others See You?**

I read a book by Myles Munroe – in it, he said: "You dress the way you want to be addressed." It was like a flashlight went off in my head.

Rightly or wrongly, people make judgements based on how you look.

The moment I got that into my mind, I started to dress a certain way. I bought a relatively inexpensive jacket that made me look good. It didn't look cheap.

I went to Selfridges – they thought I had money because I looked like I had money. I didn't – but they were paying me attention.

Remember: people address you by the way you dress. Dress accordingly.

---

* ★ *

It Is Not What Others Say About You That Matter, It Is What You Say To Yourself That MATTERS

* ★ *

Chapter 18
Take Action

Here's a list of six things you can do to get things moving:

1. Go to places where you can find people to help you.
2. Put yourself out there – make connections with people.
3. Go for free speaking engagements.

4. Sign up for one of the many networking events available – they are vast opportunities to achieve what you want.
5. Find out where the people you aspire to be are, go there, and find out more about them.
6. Print out a complimentary card showing your name, email, phone number, and aspirational job.

I have done these things since I first realised my true vocation was to be a motivational speaker.

You also have to stand out, so that when you meet the people who can help you, they will remember you.

Think of things that will differentiate you from the crowd – maybe the colour of your shoes or your glasses, your style of dressing. Make sure you leave something with them, such as your business card.

When you go somewhere, be an uplifting person. Speak with passion. They'll remember your energy, the energy you bring to people.

At a meeting with my boss, he said, "Jimmy, you've got a bubbly personality."

That's powerful – it shows I have a lot of energy.

Action Does Not Always Lead To Happiness, But

You Can't Get Happiness Without Action.

You Can Make It,
DON'T
GIVE UP

Summary

If there is one overarching message contained within this book, it is this:

Don't doubt yourself.

If there is one thing you can start using straight away, on a daily basis – or as frequently as you need to hear it – it is this simple mantra:

I am good enough;
I can do this;
I believe in myself.

The next thing you need is a plan.

Remember, planning makes dreams possible, action makes them reality.

Within your plan, incorporate the eleven essential elements of the blueprint to bring out the best in you, focusing on each of the four specific areas:

- Get to know yourself
- Set yourself up to succeed
- Step into your power
- Be bold and embrace your dream

Identify the thing that makes you truly light up, and pursue it with everything you have. Work out how to monetise it, so that you don't only help others, you also help yourself, by creating an income.

Seek out people who can help you – ask them, be positive, and be memorable.

And always remember, you don't need to be perfect – you only need to be you. Aim to be the best version of you and to live your best life. Success and fulfilment are within your grasp.

Good luck, and I hope you enjoy the journey!

Become A Confident Person

I have prepared a special Masterclass for you called:

Dare To Be Imperfect

so that you can start practicing the techniques I spoke about in the book.

Watch the **FREE** masterclass here:

www.jimmyasuni.com/masterclass

Speaking Engagements

You can book me for speaking engagements at hello@jimmyasuni.com

Strategic Alliances

If you have a business proposal or joint venture idea to collaborate with me, please email me at hello@jimmyasuni.com

Reviews:

I would highly appreciate a review on amazon.

Social Media:

Become Part Of "**Dare To Be Imperfect**" Facebook Group and find out the latest strategies to live a bolder, happier, more exciting life, free of the need to be perfect.

Follow me on social media and let me know which techniques from this book have worked for you or your business.

Follow me on Linkedin: Jimmy Asuni

Follow me on Facebook: Jimmy Asuni

Follow me on Instagram: @JimmyAsuni

Printed in Poland
by Amazon Fulfillment
Poland Sp. z o.o., Wrocław

54077689R00098